D0939085

IMAGES
of America

CHICAGO BLUES

ON THE COVER: Russell Lee took this photograph on April 6, 1941, at Tony's Tavern. Located at Thirty-first and Federal Streets in Chicago, the heart of a neighborhood called Bronzeville, Tony's Tavern opened around 1900. Its owner, Tony Finkelstein, hosted some music legends—Louis Armstrong, Cab Calloway, Duke Ellington, and Estelle and Jimmy Yancey. Menu specialties of the house were gumbo, fried shrimp, and hot dogs. Although big-name jazz and blues performers were often showcased at Tony's Tavern, lesser-known groups were also welcome, such as the one shown here. The painted mural of Walt Disney's Snow White and the Seven Dwarfs was used as an identity backdrop for photograph sessions. (Library of Congress.)

IMAGES
of America

CHICAGO BLUES

Wilbert Jones

Foreword by Kevin Johnson

ARCADIA
PUBLISHING

Published by Arcadia Publishing
Charleston, South Carolina

Library of Congress Control Number: 2014931244

For all general information, please contact Arcadia Publishing:
Telephone 843-853-2070
Fax 843-853-0044
E-mail sales@arcadiapublishing.com
For customer service and orders:
Toll-Free 1-888-313-2665

Visit us on the Internet at www.arcadiapublishing.com

Chicago Blues is dedicated to the millions of African Americans who uprooted their lives in the South and moved to Northern and Western cities across America during what became the Great Migration. They came with their skills, trade, talent, hopes, and dreams to create a better life for themselves and their families. Some of the migrants used their musical talent, which provided the foundation of rewarding America and the rest of the world with great music, such as blues.

Thank you!

CONTENTS

FOREWORD

I find it an absolutely fascinating fact that the vast majority of the most influential African American bluesmen and women in history all come from the same area of our country—the Mississippi Delta. A great deal of the older-generation Chicago bluesmen/women working today grew up in this Delta region and since moving north have developed such a powerful and distinctive style of playing. When this raw, hypnotic, and moaning country blues of Mississippi transitioned to the big city of Chicago, this emotionally intense music became even more exciting—with electricity, energy, aggression, and power. Many people think the blues is a sad, downtrodden, cry-in-your-beer type of music. Although it can be perceived that way, to many the opposite rings true: it is the most uplifting, escape-from-your-troubles-and-worries, upbeat party music that can invigorate, inspire, and touch your soul more deeply than most anything else.

The first time I really heard this exotic, mysterious music, I was hooked and needed to know more and more about this music that hit me so hard and wouldn't let go. Even though these larger-than-life blues characters now reminded me of the superheroes from the comic books and/ or the sports stars from the baseball cards I collected in my youth, I have found blues musicians to be the most down-to-earth, genuine, friendly, social, and approachable out of all musicians I have experienced.

As you can tell from the gorgeous and striking images in this important new book, the blues can and should be such a visually stimulating form of art as well. The blues star has always dressed in immaculate attire with matching colorful suits, shoes and hats, or dresses, wearing something distinctive to stand apart and entertain the crowd. This book shows fascinating images of blues history, including many superstars of both yesterday's and today's scene. I'm particularly ecstatic that it also sheds light on some of the lesser-known but equally talented musicians, some of the unsung heroes of the blues scene that deserve more recognition and attention.

Like I do, I hope you find this book and its images a vital addition to the important ongoing documentation of one of America's greatest and influential art forms—the blues!

—Kevin Johnson, director of promotions for Chicago's Delmark Records

ACKNOWLEDGMENTS

Thanks go to the following friends and colleagues and institutions who offered an abundance of support, knowledge, and research, all of which made this book possible: City of Chicago Department of Special Events, Library of Congress, Pamela J. Cash, Barry Dolins, Regina Frazer, Antoinette Simpson, Donna Hodge, Kevin Johnson at Delmark Records, Russell Lewis at the Chicago History Museum, Samuel Hernandez, Coahoma County Tourism, Bernard Loyd, Ralph Metcalf Jr., Hammons and Associates, Inc., Ann Arbor District Library, B.B. King Museum, WROX Museum, Official White House Photos (Bob Mehr), Tim Sumerel, and Maggie Bullwinkel.

INTRODUCTION

Blues was born in the fields of the Southern states around the end of the 19th century. Before blues, there were other types of singing in the fields. The physical work was next to unbearable, but the spiritual songs inspired by the Bible helped the field hands get through the long workdays.

Field hands were mostly African American. Many of them were first- and second-generation freedmen following the abolishment of slavery. Unequal wages and unfair work practices were enforced by the landowners. During this period, a partnership between the field hands and the landowners was created, called sharecropping. Under this agreement, the tenants (field hands) were allowed to use land in return for a share of the profits produced on the land. As the South became more polarized and segregated with the strengthening of Jim Crow laws, sharecroppers were subjected to more harsh and unfair practices, such as an established credit system. In one example of this process, a credit line was established and given to the sharecropper to purchase food and supplies. Once the crops were harvested, the landowner deducted the price of these expenses, which were costly—ranging from one-half to three-fourths of the profits from the crops. The cost was even higher if the sharecropper lived on the landowner's property.

During the early part of the 20th century, unions were formed to help undo some of the unfair practices enforced upon sharecroppers. One of the largest unions was the Southern Tenant Farmers Union, which included both blacks and whites. As membership grew, many landowners who had become very wealthy and politically powerful sought to dismantle these unions, which resulted in frequent violence, terror, and even the eviction of tenants from the landowner's property.

With few options for securing a safe and prosperous life in the South, sharecroppers and other African Americans who worked menial jobs, such as housekeepers, maids, cooks, nannies, butlers, and chauffeurs, decided to take their chances and move to the North. Northern cities offered industrial and manufacturing jobs that paid well. From the early 1900s to the early 1970s, millions of African Americans moved north. This event was called the Great Migration.

Northern cities were just as segregated as was the South. This was a rude awaking to many African Americans. On the other hand, these segregated communities thrived, with better educational institutions, retail stores, entertainment venues, and, to some extent, housing.

Chicago was a major destination because of its plentiful jobs as well its communities and neighborhoods, although they, too, were segregated.

Chicago's Bronzeville, which had the nickname "Black Metropolis," was a thriving African American community. It attracted the wealthy, working-class, and the poor. Although these residents lived on different blocks and in different buildings, according to social status, all socialized at the same places. Bronzeville was a mecca for blues musicians.

Many blues singers and musicians from the South, especially the Mississippi Delta, came to Chicago. The word spread fast about the city's better opportunities to make a living as a blues singer. The large number of taverns, nightclubs, bars, and other venues were looking for talent.

Blues greats who came from the Mississippi Delta included Elmore James, Muddy Waters, Leroy Foster, B.B. King, Magic Slim, Willie Dixon, Otis Spann, Sonny Boy Williamson II, Big Walter Horton, James Cotton, Jimmy Rogers, Junior Parker, Smoky Babe, Bo Diddley, Little Johnny Jones, Howlin' Wolf, and Junior Wells. They help define what is known as Chicago blues today. Also contributing were blues greats who were not from the Mississippi Delta, such as Jimmy and Estelle Yancey, Tampa Red, Big Bill Broonzy, Buddy Guy, Koko Taylor, and Earl Hooker.

Chicago blues is often described as Mississippi Delta blues supplemented with harmonica, electric guitar, drums, bass guitar, piano, and saxophone. Beyond Bronzeville, blues musicians would gather on Maxwell Street and perform. Maxwell Street is a Chicago neighborhood located on the Near West Side. It is famous for two things: the Maxwell Street Polish sandwich and the Chicago blues, both of which were said to be created there. Maxwell Street, one of the oldest parts of Chicago, predates the 1850s, about 20 years before the Great Chicago Fire. For generations, it was populated by Eastern Europeans. Then, in the early 1920s, African Americans from the Mississippi Delta started moving into the neighborhood. For decades, the Maxwell Street Market was the center of this neighborhood and one of the largest open-air markets in the country. In today's time, it would be called a flea market. Being an open-air market was an advantage for the blues performers. Greats such as Big Bill Broonzy, Jim Brewer, and a host of others used the electric guitar and amplifier. Later, the amplifier would be popularized by Bo Diddley, Muddy Waters, and Howlin' Wolf. This technique would be embraced by many other performers.

In 1994, this market was relocated, due to the expansion of the University of Illinois at Chicago. In 2008, it was moved again and renamed the New Maxwell Street Market. It remains in the same neighborhood today.

Chicago became the home of several record labels. Bluebird Records, Chess Records, Cobra Records, Delmark Records, and Alligator Records signed many blues performers. Larger labels such as Columbia and Paramount, with larger distribution networks, helped the blues draw a global audience.

One

Birth of the Blues in the Mississippi Delta

Partying on Saturday and Praying on Sunday

During Reconstruction, millions of freed slaves stayed in the South and worked as sharecroppers on plantations. Among the ways to ease the backbreaking work in the fields was singing. When slavery was legal, they sang spiritual and freedom-seeking songs. Many of these songs were passages and messages from the Bible, taught by their pastors and church leaders. The spiritual and freedom songs were sung with passion, often expressing hope for a bright future in an unjust world. Some spirituals, such as "Just a Little Talk with Jesus," "His Eye Is on the Sparrow," and "Babylon's Falling," were symbolic.

Attending church was a way to seek spiritual and emotional food for the soul. Church leaders shared their teachings, telling their congregations that life on Earth is short and that heaven lasts forever; and that if they obeyed the teachings of the Bible, they would have everlasting life upon entering the pearly gates of heaven, where the streets are paved with gold.

Many of these spiritual songs evolved into what were called work songs, which had a call-and-response structure. They were very similar to how many church programs are structured today. These work songs often described the miserable work of being a sharecropper and the bad living conditions they had to endure. In turn, some of the spirituals served as messages during the civil rights movement. One of the most popular of these songs was "Ain't Gonna Let Nobody Turn Me 'Round."

When sharecroppers were not working in the fields, they sought some type of entertainment, usually at a local juke joint. Typical entertainment included local blues musicians, many of whom worked in the same fields, on plantations, as sharecroppers. On Saturday nights, voices could be heard singing about the hard life of sharecropping, the struggle to keep a decent roof over their heads, and attempts to fix romantic relationships. The messages in the music were powerful and relatable. During the early part of the 20th century, many of the local blues musicians became celebrities within their communities. They would travel from plantations, to towns, to Southern cities, promoting their talent. Some them made a great living performing, and a few became very wealthy.

Before their names were displayed on theater marquees and billboards around the world, many blues artists began singing gospel songs in the church. Photographer Dorothea Lange captured on film this Greenville, Mississippi, church for the Farm Security Administration in July 1936. (Library of Congress.)

After long hours in the fields, sharecroppers piled themselves in wagons and sang spiritual and blues songs on the way back to their homes. The songs they sang were a reflection of their work day. (Library of Congress.)

From dawn to dusk, Monday through Friday, sharecroppers worked the fields. They sang songs that were symbolically linked to their unfair living conditions. Saturday was the only day of the week for some sort of entertainment. Sundays were reserved for church. (Library of Congress.)

Many music historians believe that the blues was born in the cotton fields of the Mississippi Delta. The genre is believed to have derived from gospel, chants, and work songs. (Library of Congress.)

Picking cotton by hand was painful work. Blues musician Lead Belly (Huddie William Ledbetter, 1888–1949) recorded the song "Cotton Fields" in 1940. The lyrics were about his experience working in the cotton fields of Louisiana. (Library of Congress.)

Entire families often worked together in the fields, including children. During these difficult times, attending school was not the highest priority. Keeping a roof over their heads and putting food on the table and clothes on their backs were the primary concerns. (Library of Congress.)

When sharecroppers organized and joined unions, landowners hired day laborers to work their land. Day laborers were less of an investment for the landowners. Sharecroppers who also performed as blues musicians sang at house parties, on street corners, and in juke joints to generate more income. (Library of Congress.)

Day laborers who picked cotton were often paid by the pound. Later, they were paid by the hour, which still left field hands overworked and underpaid. These practices led day laborers and field hands to start singing work and blues songs. (Library of Congress.)

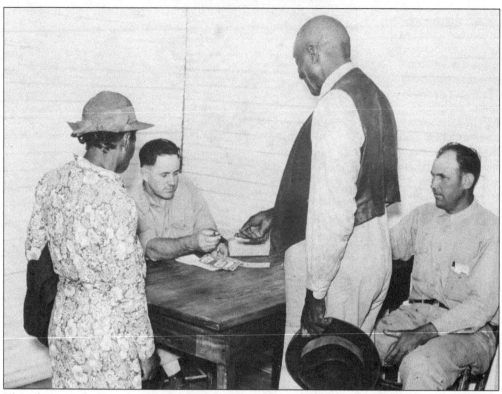

This photograph was taken on Good Hope Plantation in the Mississippi Delta in the 1940s. It shows sharecroppers getting paid on a Saturday afternoon by the plantation manager. With the little monies received, some sharecroppers still managed to save earnings, which was often spent at the local juke joint and/or church. (Library of Congress.)

Nearly every plantation operated a store, where groceries and supplies could be purchased on a credit system. These stores often charged outrageous markups, which yielded great profits for the plantation owner. (Library of Congress.)

During the 1940s and 1950s, women were often hired as day laborers to work landowners' crops because they could often be paid less than men. These women earned less than $1 a day, and no profits from the crops were shared with them. This photograph was taken by Marion Post Wolcott in June 1940 on the Hopson Plantation near Clarksdale, Mississippi. (Library of Congress.)

Plantation field managers, who handled the details of the sharecroppers and day laborers, lived in large and elaborate homes, such as the one shown in this photograph. (Library of Congress.)

Plantation owners lived in some of the most beautiful homes in America. During the early part of the 20th century, blues musicians often wrote about the unfair world they lived in, working as sharecroppers, field hands, and at other menial jobs. (Library of Congress.)

One of the Mississippi Delta's wealthiest plantation owners was the King and Anderson family. They were called King of Cotton. The commodity was so important to the family that nearly all of its 17,000-acre property was dedicated to cotton. This photograph shows cotton growing on all sides of the family's private cemetery. (Library of Congress.)

This is a typical sharecropper's house on the King and Anderson plantation. A home was loaned to a sharecropper as long as he or she picked cotton and stayed out of political activities that would benefit sharecroppers. (Library of Congress.)

Shown here is a sharecropper's home on the wealthy Knowlton Plantation in Mississippi. Living conditions for sharecroppers were the same throughout the South. The disparity in incomes and amenities between the landowners and sharecroppers was great. (Library of Congress.)

Local juke joints were always packed on Saturday evenings. Amateur and professional blues artists worked these establishments, where music, dancing, drinking, eating, and, sometimes, gambling occurred. Plantation workers and sharecroppers came to socialize and enjoy themselves after a long work week in the fields. (Library of Congress.)

Juke joints were not just places to listen to great music; they were also great dance clubs. Delta blues musician John Ned "Johnny" Shines (1915–1992) is quoted as saying, "You mostly played for the dancers." (Library of Congress.)

Some owners and operators of juke joints generated extra income by hosting gambling parties and selling moonshine in their establishments. Moonshine is a high-proof distilled homemade whiskey, usually made from corn or potatoes. It was often sold illegally during the early and middle years of the 20th century. (Both, Library of Congress.)

Barbershops located throughout the Mississippi Delta welcomed blues musicians into their establishments. Customers, like the men shown here, would often sit outside to meet and greet the musicians before they performed. (Library of Congress.)

Blues fans come from around the world to take a photograph of themselves standing at this intersection, located outside of Clarksdale, Mississippi. It was rumored that blues musician Robert Johnson (1911–1938) sold his soul to the devil at this crossroads; he had a burning desire to become a great blues musician. According to legend, he was told by the devil to bring his guitar to the intersection of highways 61 and 49 in the Mississippi Delta. The devil took Johnson's guitar, tuned it, played a few songs, then gave it back to Johnson. The bluesman became the master of his guitar, but for only a few short years. He was given the titles King of the Delta Blues and Father of Rock 'n' Roll. On August 16, 1938, Johnson died. Some close friends believed he was poisoned by drinking a bad bottle of moonshine. (Hammons and Associates, Inc.)

Bessie Smith (1892–1937), known as The Empress of the Blues, was born in Chattanooga, Tennessee. Her career peaked during the 1920s and 1930s. She signed with Columbia Records in 1923 and produced a series of so-called race records, which were marketed to the African American community. (Library of Congress, Prints and Photographs Division, Carl Van Vechten Collection, Reproduction Number LC-USZ62-54231.)

During the 1920s and 1930s, Bessie Smith was one of the richest women in America. One of her biggest records, "Crazy Blues," recorded in 1920 for Okeh Records, sold over 100,000 copies in one month. (Library of Congress, Prints and Photographs Division, Carl Van Vechten Collection, Reproduction Number LC-USZ62-94955.)

On September 26, 1937, Bessie Smith died in a car accident while traveling between Memphis, Tennessee, and Clarksdale, Mississippi. Rumors circulated throughout the country about her being denied admission to a whites-only hospital in Clarksdale, which was closer to where the accident occurred. She was transferred to the G.T. Thomas Afro-American Hospital, where she died. In 1944, the hospital was turned into the Riverside Hotel.

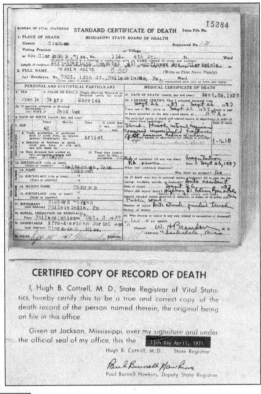

CERTIFIED COPY OF RECORD OF DEATH

I, Hugh B. Cottrell, M. D., State Registrar of Vital Statistics, hereby certify this to be a true and correct copy of the death record of the person named therein, the original being on file in this office.

Given at Jackson, Mississippi, over my signature and under the official seal of my office, this the 13th Day April, 1971

Hugh B. Cottrell, M.D.   State Registrar

Paul Burnell Hawkins, Deputy State Registrar

Shown here is the Riverside Hotel. For decades, it was Clarksdale's only lodging that accepted African Americans. Notable guests included Robert Nighthawk, Sonny Boy Williamson, and Ike Turner. (Coahoma County Tourism.)

Wade Walton was a blues musician who recorded one hit record, in 1958, titled "Shake 'Em on Down." The song was widely distributed throughout Europe. Wade opened an establishment in Clarksdale, which was called a barbershop juke joint. On Saturday afternoons, lucky customers would come for haircuts and watch some of the greatest blues artists perform, including B.B. King, Muddy Waters, John Lee Hooker, and Ike Turner. (Coahoma County Tourism.)

The Delta Blues Museum, located in Clarksdale, Mississippi, opened in 1979. Wade Walton's barbershop chair and the remains of the cabin where Muddy Waters lived during his days as a sharecropper are displayed in the gallery of this museum. (Coahoma County Tourism.)

In 1944, the Hopson Plantation was one of the first cotton plantations to use a mechanical cotton-picker. Today, the commissary, along with the remaining buildings on the property, has been turned into a tourist destination including lodging on-site. (Coahoma County Tourism.)

This photograph, taken in October 1939, captures a typical Saturday afternoon in the Mississippi Delta. Although segregation laws were tightly enforced, both African Americans and whites shopped at the same large department and grocery stores, seeking better and more variety of products. (Library of Congress.)

Blues musicians wrote songs about the challenges of picking cotton and living on plantations. This photograph shows sharecroppers' homes surrounded by cotton plants. The hard work and industry was a day-to-day reality, next to impossible to escape. (Library of Congress.)

After cotton was harvested, sharecroppers had the task of taking samples to the local broker's office in town to negotiate commodity market prices. This banker's office was located in downtown Clarksdale, Mississippi. The photograph was taken around 1939. (Library of Congress.)

Local brokers usually paid African American sharecroppers a fraction of the commodity price, less than what white sharecroppers received. These practices continued until unions were formed to help create a fairer pay scale. (Library of Congress.)

After a long week of working in the fields, laborers would congregate outside of local cafés, barbershops, and juke joints to wait for blues performers to entertain them. (Library of Congress.)

This photograph was taken in 1939 in Belzoni, Mississippi. Field-workers relax and wait for the local African American–owned café across the road to open its doors for an evening of entertainment. (Library of Congress.)

This is a typical juke joint, made of tin siding and discarded parts from torn-down sharecroppers' homes. Although they were far from fancy, these establishments hosted some of the greatest blues musicians, including Muddy Waters, B.B. King, Robert Nighthawk, Elmore James, and many others. (Library of Congress.)

A crowd in downtown Clarksdale, Mississippi, waits for local blues street musicians to perform. This concept would take musicians to large cities such as Chicago for more money and a bigger audience. (Library of Congress.)

Due to the unfair pay they received for their work, African Americans learned how to stretch their money, purchasing used clothes, shoes, and household goods from white vendors. Blues musicians purchased used clothes and instruments in pursuit of their performing careers. (Library of Congress.)

Shown here is the convergence of two different worlds in the South. Few African Americans in the South owned cars in the 1940s, when this photograph was taken. They either undertook long walks or traveled by wagons and horses to town to do their weekend shopping or enjoy local entertainment. (Library of Congress.)

Before fast-food restaurant chains were established and popularized, small cafés such as the one shown here operated throughout the South. These cafés served food that was easy to prepare and inexpensive. This photograph shows a menu posted outside of the café. Urging folks to "come in & eat," the menu includes fried pies, ham sandwiches, hot dogs, and fish. (Library of Congress.)

Some juke joints offered customers a place to enjoy music, dance, eat, and gamble. Owners made extra money by selling groceries and moonshine. Children often hung around outside of juke joints, looking for adults to give them a little pocket change. (Library of Congress.)

Muddy Waters (McKinley Morganfield, 1913–1983) was born in the Mississippi Delta. At the age of 17, he earned money by playing the harmonica and guitar at house parties and juke joints. In 1943, he moved to Chicago and became a full-time blues musician. One of his mentors, Big Bill Broonzy, who was a leading bluesman in Chicago, allowed Muddy Waters to open his shows. At that time, clubs were packed and featured great musical competitions. (Ann Arbor District Library.)

Muddy Waters's career transformed him into one of the most well-respected blues musicians in the world. However, he never forgot his humble beginnings; he continued to sing Delta and Chicago-inspired blues, recording over 500 songs. Muddy Waters won multiple Grammys and was inducted into the Rock and Roll Hall of Fame. Many blues experts credit him with giving birth to rock 'n' roll music. (Chicago History Museum.)

Another Mississippi Delta musician who influenced the blues industry, especially Chicago blues, was Riley "B.B." King. He was born on September 16, 1925, on a cotton plantation outside of Berclair, Mississippi. He started playing the guitar for local churches when he was 12. At the age of 17, he became a tractor driver to generate more income. In 1949, King began recording blues songs and toured the entire chitlin circuit—the name given to the series of performance venues throughout America that were safe and acceptable for African American musicians, comedians, and other entertainers during segregation. (B.B. King Museum.)

B.B. King rose to the top of his career, receiving the Presidential Medal of Freedom on December 15, 2006, presented by Pres. George W. Bush. This award is considered one of the highest honors given by a sitting president. (Official White House Photo, Bob Mehr.)

The Mississippi State Penitentiary, also known as Parchman Farm, became the home of many workers and sharecroppers who tried to fight segregation, unfair work policies, and daily discrimination. However, even when they were locked up, they kept singing. The late blues and soul singer Sam Cooke produced one of his biggest records, "Chain Gang," in 1960. It describes the harsh conditions of imprisoned men working all day long under unacceptable conditions. (Mississippi Department of Archives and History.)

The Parchman Penal Farm for female prisoners, also located in the Mississippi Delta, operated in the same manner as did the men's prison. Inmates were forced to work on private and state-owned farms, receiving no payment or compensation. This photograph shows a group of female prisoners making their uniforms. (Mississippi Department of Archives and History.)

In the mid-1940s, due to rising tension between workers and landowners, and with the Great Migration in full swing, Mexican Americans and immigrants were encouraged to come and work as sharecroppers. Wealthy landowners and plantation managers reached out to this other source of labor. (Library of Congress.)

During the peak of cotton harvesting, the entire family was expected to help. This photograph shows a Mexican American family working together. (Library of Congress.)

After experiencing years of discrimination and financial hardship, millions of African Americans packed their belongings and left the plantations and cotton fields. (Library of Congress.)

A new beginning: "We have had enough and cannot make it here." These thoughts were uppermost in the minds of many African Americans who decided to uproot their lives in the South to seek better living conditions in the North, including Chicago—the promised land. (Library of Congress.)

Two

THE GREAT MIGRATION
SWEET HOME CHICAGO!

Between the early 1900s and the mid-1970s, more than six million African Americans moved from the rural South to cities in the Midwest, the Northeast, and in western parts of the United States. Many of these migrants ended up making Chicago's South Side and West Side neighborhoods their new homes.

Some of those who left the Mississippi Delta and traveled to Chicago did so via the Illinois Central's (IC) sister passenger train, the Yazoo & Mississippi Valley Railroad. It covered more than 800 miles and went throughout the Mississippi Delta, stopping in nearly every tiny town.

Pullman porters who worked on the trains offered more than the standard passenger services. They passed out copies of the *Chicago Defender*, one of the most respected African American newspapers in America. The paper included announcements and advertisements of organized migrant clubs, discount group travel rates, industry job postings, and housing rental information for passengers traveling north.

The famous song "Sweet Home Chicago" was written and recorded by Robert Johnson in November 1936. Although he never moved to Chicago, he, along with other blues musicians, often talked about that great promised land, where jobs were plentiful and Jim Crow laws were not as rigid as they were in the South.

Other blues greats recorded and sang signature songs about Chicago. Jimmy Rogers (1924–1997) recorded "Chicago Bound," and Arthur "Big Boy" Crudup (1905–1974) recorded "The Greatest Place Around." Both Rogers and Crudup made Chicago their home. They were able to experience firsthand what the so-called promised land was really like. Many blues experts believe that, if Robert Johnson's life had not been cut short, he, too, would have moved to the Windy City.

As time passed, many Northern cities became overcrowded. Segregation policies and housing restrictions were enforced. African American communities became extremely congested and experienced high crime levels. Many spacious apartments and homes were turned into small kitchenettes, and entire families would make them their homes. There were also a host of boardinghouses, which were large homes cut up to make individual bedrooms. The bathrooms and kitchens were considered common areas and were shared by tenants. The slogan for the promised land became "All Glitter Ain't Gold." And blues musicians started to sing about it.

The Yazoo & Mississippi Valley Railroad served nearly every small town throughout the Mississippi Delta. Thousands of African Americans used this train line to come to Chicago and other large cities. This photograph captures a great view of the train crossing the Illinois Central Gulf Railroad Bridge outside of Vicksburg, Mississippi. (Library of Congress.)

This is the Illinois Central Railroad hub, located in the heart of downtown Chicago, across from Lake Michigan. It was considered the Great Migration's version of Ellis Island. The Illinois Central was a major carrier of passenger and freight trains out of the South. (Library of Congress.)

In the background of this photograph are row houses, built in the Grand Boulevard community on Chicago's South Side for the wealthy during the late 1800s. African Americans started to move in around the early part of the 20th century. The community was renamed Bronzeville, nicknamed the "Black Metropolis." (Library of Congress.)

In a few decades' time, Bronzeville became a true promised land. As the wealthy moved out, African Americans purchased their mansions, row houses, grand apartments, and commercial businesses. The neighborhood also included an abundance of African American role models—doctors, lawyers, educators, religious leaders, business owners, and top-notch performing artists. (Library of Congress.)

Children enjoyed the freedom of playing in their neighborhood without the fear of harm or danger. Those of their parents who had lived in the South as children had not been not as fortunate. (Library of Congress.)

Blues musician Big Bill Broonzy (1893–1958) moved to Chicago in the early 1920s, during the Great Migration. His career started with country blues, but he transitioned to urban blues. During his lifetime, he recorded and copyrighted over 300 songs. In the early 1950s, he reinvented himself by becoming part of a folk music tour in Europe. Broonzy, a mentor to Muddy Waters, also influenced Memphis Slim, Ray Davies, Rory Gallagher, and Steve Howe. (Chicago History Museum.)

Big Bill Broonzy (left) enjoyed performing at small clubs throughout the country. This photograph was taken in 1957 at a club in Chicago's Old Town neighborhood. (Chicago History Museum.)

From the early part of the 20th century until the 1940s, Chicago's Bronzeville neighborhood was considered a promised land. Its streets were lined with successful businesses owned by African Americans. Doctors and lawyers set up their practices along vibrant Forty-seventh Street. Madame C.J. Walker, one of American's first African American millionaires, had a successful beauty school in this neighborhood. (Library of Congress.)

Before there were 7-Eleven and White Hen Pantry chains, small convenience stores were located on almost every corner in urban neighborhoods. They were filled with fresh and perishable foods and household products. (Library of Congress.)

The A&P grocery store was one of the few businesses in Bronzeville not owned by African Americans. The goods stocked at this store included what the community wanted to buy, not what they had to buy. (Library of Congress.)

The Regal Theater located at Forty-seventh Street and South Parkway was one of the most prominent entertainment establishments in America. It was built in 1928. Some of the most recognized African American entertainers graced its stage over its 50 years, from Josephine Baker to B.B. King. (Library of Congress.)

The architecture firm Levy and Klein designed the original Regal Theater (pictured). Its design was influenced by New York City's Savoy Ballroom, which was located in Harlem. The Regal was one of the few elegant and formal places that admitted African American customers. Sadly, it was torn down in 1973. Years later, the Avalon Theater, located at 1641 East Seventy-ninth Street, was renovated and renamed the New Regal Theater. The 2,300-seat theater has flipped ownership several times. In 2014, it was sold for a mere $100,000. Its future is still up in the air. Some community leaders would like to see it turned into a culture center or a visitor information center. (Library of Congress.)

The Savoy Ballroom was located next door to the Regal Theater, at 4733 South Park Way. It opened in 1927. Originally, most of its featured performers were jazz artists, including Louis Armstrong, Count Basie, Duke Ellington, and Ella Fitzgerald. Eventually, blues greats such as Howlin' Wolf (Chester Arthur Burnett) and Elmore James performed at the Savoy. (Chicago History Museum.)

The Savoy Ballroom was also used to host basketball events, figure skating competitions, comedy acts, cabaret shows, and awards programs. (Chicago History Museum.)

For decades, the Savoy Ballroom was one of the most popular venues in Chicago. It hosted some of the biggest entertainers. This photograph captures a typical Saturday evening: a full house inside the Savoy in 1941. The venue closed in 1948 and was demolished in 1973. (Chicago History Museum.)

The partying continued after entertainers finished their performances. Here, Lead Belly (right) and folk musician Woody Guthrie play in Steven Dutchman's apartment in 1941. Lead Belly (Huddie William Ledbetter, 1888–1949) wrote and sang songs that touched on the newsmakers of his time, including Franklin D. Roosevelt, Adolf Hitler, the Scottsboro Boys, and Howard Hughes. He played Delta blues, country blues, and folk music. (Chicago History Museum.)

By 1940, Bronzeville's population had grown to more than 300,000. There were more nightclubs and dance halls in this neighborhood than in downtown Chicago. Jazz and blues musicians from across the country recognized Bronzeville as their promised land. (Library of Congress.)

This intersection of Forty-fourth and State Streets was once considered the center of the Black Metropolis, second only to New York City's Harlem neighborhood. Bronzeville was one of the best urban, social, cultural, and economic neighborhoods in the world. (Library of Congress.)

Arthur "Big Boy" Crudup (1905–1974) came to Chicago in 1939 and worked as a solo guitar Delta blues performer in several clubs and taverns on Chicago's South Side and West Side. Among his signature songs were "That's All Right," "My Baby Left Me," and "So Glad You Are Mine." (Chicago History Museum.)

During the 1950s Crudup was one of the pioneers who stopped recording and making records because of the battle over royalties and the small wages he received as a singer and songwriter. (Chicago History Museum.)

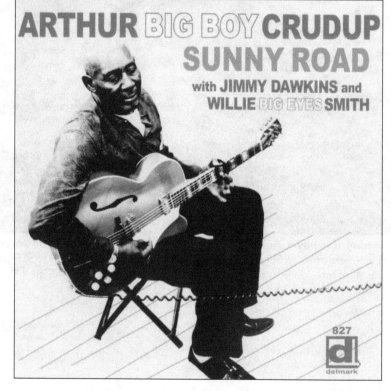

Arthur Crudup went back into the studios in the mid-1960s and recorded songs for Fire Records and Delmark Records. He worked until the early 1970s. One of his last tours was a trip to the United Kingdom, where he recorded "Roebuck Man" with local musicians. (Delmark Records.)

The Union Stock Yards was one of the largest employers in the country. It helped Chicago earn the nickname "Hog Butcher for the World." Thousands of African Americans worked there, including many blues musicians. The stockyards opened in 1885 and closed in 1971. (Library of Congress.)

African American entrepreneurship was prominent in their communities during the Great Migration. It was important for African Americans to spend their money at businesses that treated them with respect. Segregated stores throughout the South would not let African Americans try out merchandise before deciding to purchase it. This African American bank serviced the community. (Library of Congress.)

The African American Chas. F. Gardner store, located at 2933 South State Street, was one of the best repair and hardware stores in Chicago. (Library of Congress.)

Hat shops, such as Pete's Expert Shop, not only sold and repaired hats, they also performed custom tailoring and clothes-pressing services. (Library of Congress.)

The Ida B. Wells Homes, a Chicago public housing project, was built in 1939–1941. The development's aim was to relieve overcrowding and replace dilapidated housing in Bronzeville. There were 1,662 units built, a combination of row houses and mid- and high-rise apartment buildings. The site was located between Thirty-seventh and Thirty-ninth Streets, boarded by what became Martin Luther King Jr. Drive and Cottage Grove. (Library of Congress.)

DEDICATION CEREMONIES

IDA B. WELLS HOMES
38½ ST. *and* RHODES
Sunday, OCTOBER 27½ 1940
· · · 2:30 P.M · · ·
Parade along South Parkway 1:00 p.m.

HON. EDW. J. KELLY *Mayor* · · · SPEAKER

CHICAGO HOUSING AUTHORITY

Lunch wagons were popular throughout Bronzeville. This concept was considered fast food on wheels. Vendors sold food that was easy to prepare and sell—pies, hot dogs, fresh fruit, and beverages. (Library of Congress.)

One of Chicago's most important buildings for African Americans was the Wabash Avenue YMCA, located at 3763 South Wabash Avenue. The residents of Bronzeville and Julius Rosenwald, the president of Sears, Roebuck and Co., raised $75,000 to erect this building. It opened on June 15, 1915, and immediately offered services—including helping residents find housing, education programs, vocational training, and health care. Organized groups, such as music clubs, Bible study groups, sports teams, and health campaigns held events at this location. In 1970, the Wabash Avenue YMCA closed due to the decline in the neighborhood. In 2000, it reopened after a $9 million renovation. This neighborhood treasure is in the National Register of Historic Places. (Library of Congress.)

Small independent stores offered pharmaceutical services in order to compete with drugstores. The registered pharmacist at this establishment distributed prescribed drugs to customers. (Library of Congress.)

One of the most renowned nightclubs in Bronzeville was Club DeLisa. It was opened in 1934 by four DeLisa brothers at 5521 South State Street. Jazz, blues, bebop, and rhythm and blues were the types of music performed. The club also hosted comedians and dance events. (Library of Congress.)

Red Saunders (1912–1981) was a drummer and bandleader at Club DeLisa. He also worked at the Regal Theater and the Savoy Ballroom. Although Saunders was known as a great jazz drummer, as a bandleader, he played other types of music, such as swing, bebop, and the blues. (Library of Congress.)

Count Basie (1904–1984) took his "bluesy" band to the Savoy Ballroom in 1938. Dance contests were frequently held there, as were battles between jazz, swing, and early blues bands. Basie's record "Swingin' the Blues" was a favorite among the fans. (Library of Congress.)

Jazz and blues drummer Oliver Coleman (1914–1965), shown in this photograph, was a regular performer at the Savoy Ballroom and the Regal Theater. (Library of Congress.)

From the first decade of the 1900s through the 1960s, there were at least two nightclubs located on nearly every commercial block in Bronzeville. During this period, lesser-known entertainers kept the doors open during the Depression and through World War II. Photographer Russell Lee (1903–1986) took this image.. (Library of Congress.)

Amateur jazz, swing, and blues groups, such as the one shown here, had the difficult task of undertaking repeated auditions before they were permanently hired by club owners and managers. (Library of Congress.)

During the early part of the 20th century, African American men frequently congregated on street corners and in front of neighborhood stores to discuss important news and neighborhood gossip. (Library of Congress.)

The Bronzeville neighborhood had successful retail stores. The merchandise sold in these establishments was of high quality, rivaling that in the big department stores located in downtown Chicago. (Library of Congress.)

Before large marquees stood in the yards of churches, simple blackboard signs were used. This image was taken by photographer Edwin Rosskam (1903–1985). (Library of Congress.)

Amateur groups sang different styles of music, and jazz and blues were always popular. Some groups, such as the one shown here, performed frequently at Tony's Tavern, which was located at Thirty-first and Federal Streets in Bronzeville. (Library of Congress.)

Joseph Lee "Big Joe" Williams (1903–1982) was a Delta blues guitarist, singer, and songwriter. He performed one of his signature songs, "Baby Please Don't Go" (Blackbird, 1935), in nearly every venue in Bronzeville and in taverns on Chicago's West Side. He would eventually take his nine-string guitar and perform in some of Europe's and Japan's largest venues. (Both, Chicago History Museum.)

Eddy "The Chief" Clearwater, also known as Edward Harrington, was born in Macon, Mississippi, in 1935. Since the 1950s, he has played an important role in Chicago's blues scene. Clearwater plays the electric guitar, and his voice has been described as hard-driving. He plays Windy City blues and acoustic country blues as well as gospel uplift. He is called "The Chief" because of the Native American headdress he sometimes wears. Clearwater was influenced by Chuck Berry, Otis Rush, and Magic Sam. (Delmark Records.)

The tradition of "partying on Saturday and praying on Sunday" has been a part of the blues culture. Most African Americans who lived in the South were Baptists. Those who migrated to the North had the option to become members of whatever religious faith was practiced in their community. In this 1941 photograph, Catholic parishioners prepare for an Easter-morning program on the South Side of Chicago. (Library of Congress.)

Within the African American community, there were many forms of religion and services. However, the spiritual songs were similar, many having been sung by churchgoers' ancestors more than a century before. (Library of Congress.)

Located at 3300 South Indiana Avenue, this building was originally a synagogue, KAM Isaiah Israel Temple, built in 1891 and designed by famed architect Louis Sullivan and engineer Dankmar Adler. In 1922, it became the Pilgrim Baptist Church. Thomas A. Dorsey, considered the father of gospel music, was the music director here. Many blues musicians call this church their spiritual home. (Library of Congress.)

Here, paperboys meet churchgoers on a Sunday afternoon in front of Pilgrim Baptist Church. Sadly, on June 6, 2006, while having its roof repaired, the building experienced a fire. Nearly all of its interior was burned, including decades of historical records and boxes of Dorsey's original sheet music. In 2010, designs were unveiled to rebuild this historic church. Some of its members included America's first black female aviator, Bessie Coleman (1892–1926); gospel singer Mahalia Jackson (1911–1972); and the first African American heavyweight boxing champion, Jack Johnson (1878–1946). (Library of Congress.)

Worshippers who attended this Pentecostal church often described its services as nourishment for the soul. This same description was given by sharecroppers who sang church songs while working cotton fields in the South. (Library of Congress.)

Pastors and ministers who left the South during the Great Migration benefited in the North by heading up larger congregations. They had more freedom to teach their religion and to expand their teachings. (Library of Congress.)

Church leaders were the pillars of the community. They took great interest in bonding with the congregation outside of the church. Family dinner invitations and private home counseling sessions were common. (Library of Congress.)

Blues artist Big Time Sarah (b. 1953) was born in Coldwater, Mississippi, and was raised in Chicago. During her early childhood, like many blues musician, Sarah sang gospel in church choirs. At the age of 14, she started singing the blues. (Delmark Records.)

Big Time Sarah has performed with Zora Young, Bonnie Lee, Buddy Guy, Magic Slim, Sunnyland Slim, and Junior Wells. She toured Europe in 1982 and recorded an album in Paris, France. (Delmark Records.)

Segregated neighborhoods on Chicago's South and West Sides became overcrowded at the peak of the Great Migration. Spacious homes and luxury apartment buildings were divided into smaller apartments and kitchenettes. Building owners charged tenants premium rents because of the relatively low supply of housing and the high demand. (Library of Congress.)

The basements and first floors of many apartment buildings in Bronzeville were converted into commercial businesses. This photograph shows a grocery store, called the It Club, in a basement. (Library of Congress.)

By the 1950s, Bronzeville had become a run-down neighborhood, one of the worst in America. Playwright Lorraine Hansberry's *A Raisin in the Sun* is based on life in this neighborhood. The play portrays an African American family's experience living in a wretched two-bedroom apartment. In 1973, *Raisin*, a musical based on Hansberry's play, won a Tony Award for Best Musical. (Library of Congress.)

In the middle of the 20th century, kitchenettes were commonly found throughout overcrowded neighborhoods. Author Richard Wright called kitchenettes "our prison, our death sentence without a trial." (Library of Congress.)

Bronzeville was transformed from a promised land to an overcrowded and unsafe area. When unemployment increased, stores, restaurants, and entertainment venues closed their doors. (Library of Congress.)

Most kitchenettes did not include private bathrooms. The apartment building shown here offered renters free gas and electricity. African Americans who had lived on plantations before coming to Chicago often described their new living conditions as less desirable than those in the South. Of course, blues musicians started to write songs and sing about the deplorable conditions in segregated communities in the North. (Library of Congress.)

As the population grew out of control in segregated African American communities, signs such as this one began to appear in nearby white neighborhoods. The building's tenants would be changing—from all white to all black. (Library of Congress.)

The *Chicago Defender*, America's most prominent African American newspaper with a national circulation, often featured articles about the challenges of housing discrimination in Chicago. (Library of Congress.)

In the 1940s, workers as well as tenants joined together and picketed against Mid City Realty, one of the largest property owners in some of the poorest Chicago neighborhoods. (Library of Congress.)

Both whites and blacks picketed and held strikes against Mid City Realty. Powerful political leaders eventually came up with a solution: tear down many of the dilapidated houses in the African American communities and replace them with high-rise public housing. This idea kept housing segregation intact. The Julian A. Black Reality Company (shown here) and other realty companies owned by African Americans helped to end housing discrimination. (Library of Congress.)

Despite the terrible living conditions in Bronzeville, some residents tried their best to beautify the neighborhood, sometimes using meager resources. (Library of Congress.)

Blues great Junior Wells (Amos Wells Blakemore Jr., 1934–1998) was born in West Memphis, Arkansas. He moved to Chicago in 1948 and worked as a blues singer at rent parties on Chicago's South and West Sides. In 1952, he made his first recording, a collaboration with Muddy Waters at Chess Records. (Delmark Records.)

At the age of seven, Junior Wells learned how to play the harmonica. He would become one of the best players in the world. During his career, Junior performed with Earl Hooker, Buddy Guy, the Rolling Stones, Van Morrison, and Bonnie Raitt. (Chicago History Museum.)

Junior Wells's *Hoodoo Man Blues* (1965, Delmark) became his best-selling album. Some blues critics rated it as his best album. (Delmark Records.)

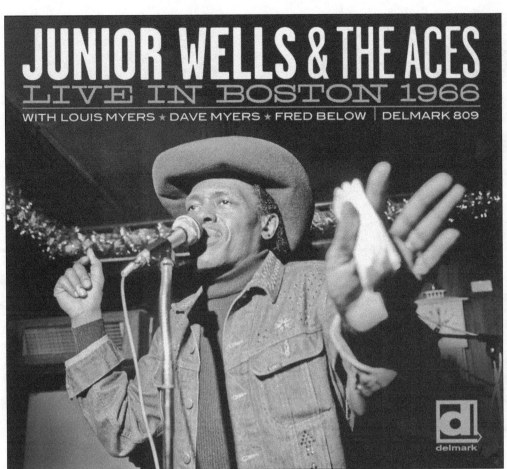

Junior Wells's career lasted over 50 years. This 1966 *Live in Boston* album, made with the Aces, remains popular today. (Delmark Records.)

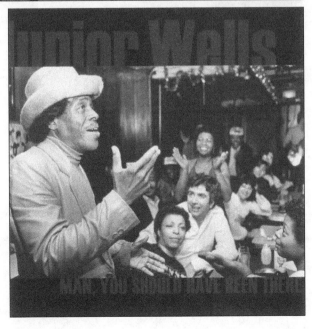

Wells's *South Side Blues Jam* album (1971, Delmark) includes a political song, "Blues for Mayor Daley." (Delmark Records.)

Maxwell Street Market was originally located between Halsted Street and Roosevelt Road, on Chicago's Near West Side. For decades, it was an economic hub for the poor. (Chicago History Museum.)

The neighborhood surrounding Maxwell Street Market was the gateway community for immigrants, including Bohemians, Germans, Greeks, Italians, Mexicans, Russians, and African Americans who migrated from the South. (Chicago History Museum.)

Maxwell Street Market is seen from above in the late 1940s, during its bustling days. Buyers were expected to barter and haggle over prices in the open-air flea market as well as inside the established stores. (Chicago History Museum.)

African American musicians who left the South brought with them outdoor music. Maxwell Street Market was the perfect venue to come and enjoy blues musicians. (Chicago History Museum.)

Magic Sam (Samuel Gene Maghett, 1937–1969) was born in Grenada, Mississippi. He learned to play the blues by listening to Muddy Waters and Little Walter records. Magic Sam moved to Chicago's West Side in 1950. He played at Maxwell Street Market, lounges, and nightclubs. (Delmark Records.)

In 1957, Magic Sam recorded his first record, "All Your Love" (Cobra Records). (Delmark Records.)

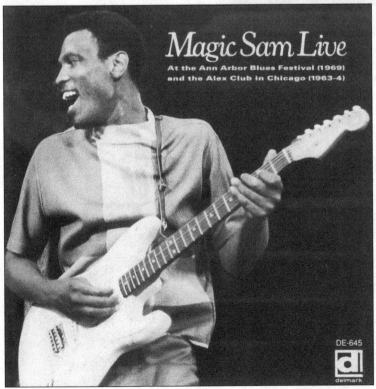

Magic Sam was known for his unique tremolo guitar playing. In 1963, he gained national exposure for his record "Feelin' Good (We're Gonna Boogie)." In 1967, Magic Sam recorded his signature album, *West Side Soul*, for Delmark. (Delmark Records.)

Sadly, Magic Sam died of a heart attack at the young age of 32. His style of guitar playing inspired and influenced many blues artists after his death. (Chicago History Museum.)

The Maxwell Street Polish sandwich is as symbolic to Chicago as Maxwell Street Market. It was created by Jimmy Stefanoic (pictured), a Macedonian immigrant who took over his aunt and uncle's hot dog stand in 1939. A Maxwell Street Polish consists of a grilled or fried Polish sausage, topped with lots of grilled onions, yellow mustard, and some optional hot sport peppers, served on a bun. (Chicago History Museum.)

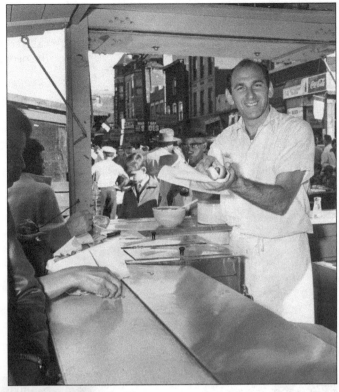

On any given day, hundreds of vendors flock to Maxwell Street Market to sell their goods. This photograph, taken in the 1960s, shows a vendor with stylish wigs and hairpieces for sale. (Chicago History Museum.)

Gospel singers came to Maxwell Street Market to perform spiritual music. They called their activity "bringing church to the people." (Chicago History Museum.)

Some performers who entertained at Maxwell Street Market were versatile. They sang blues on Saturdays and returned on Sunday afternoon to sing gospel music. (Chicago History Museum.)

Occasionally, more than singing was required in order to grab a shopper's attention. The latest dance moves helped persuade the spectators to pay for the performance. (Chicago History Museum.)

One of Chicago's best-known blues daughters is Shirley Johnson. She grew up in Virginia but has called Chicago her home since 1985. Like many blues artists, Johnson started her career singing gospel music in the church. But she always had an appreciation and love for the blues. Etta James, Bobby "Blue" Bland, and Ruth Brown were some of her favorite performers. In 2009, Johnson released the album *Blues Attack* (Delmark), which was nominated for two Blues Blast Music Awards in the Best Female Artist and Best Traditional Blues Recordings categories. That same year, Johnson headlined the opening night for the Chicago Blues Festival. (Delmark Records.)

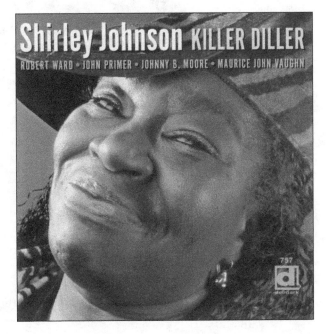

Byther Smith was born in Monticello, Mississippi, in 1933. He came to Chicago in the 1950s to play with a three-piece jazz group. Eventually, he mastered the guitar and became one of the greatest blues artists in the world. After traveling around the world several times, Byther still records and continues to tour frequently at the age of 81. (Delmark Records.)

In 1939, blues guitarist and singer Eddie C. Campbell was born in Duncan, Mississippi. He moved to Chicago in 1942. During his early career, Campbell played for Jimmy Reed, Little Johnny Taylor, Little Walter, and Howlin' Wolf. In the 1980s, Campbell moved to Europe, but he later returned to Chicago. In 2013, he suffered a stroke and heart attack while on tour, which left him paralyzed on the right side of his body. Today, he has full use of both sides of his body. (Delmark Records.)

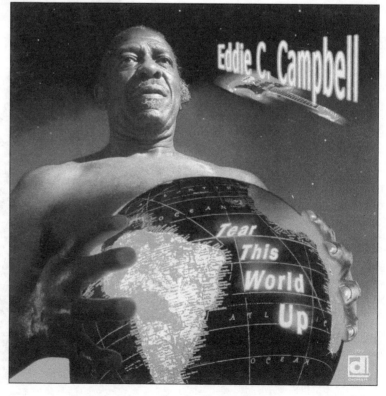

Three

GOING GLOBAL
AN INTERNATIONAL AUDIENCE

If only blues pioneer Robert Johnson could have lived to see how the inspiration of his music influenced the world of music today. Blues historians believe that rock 'n' roll, rhythm and blues, soul music, and rap came from the blues.

Blues expanded from the fields in the South and ended up on stages and venues around the world. B.B. King and Buddy Guy are known globally. Fans of every color and creed have a deep appreciation for the meaning of this music, which touches on relatable issues such as relationships and hard financial times. International fans pay homage by taking trips to the Mississippi Delta to attend blues festivals, tour Chicago's Bronzeville neighborhood, listen to street musicians at the Maxwell Street Market, and attend the Chicago Blues Festival. The city of Chicago has adopted many blues artists over the years. The late Koko Taylor was crowned the "Queen of the Blues." During the height of her career, she had a nightclub on Division Street in Chicago's Near North Side neighborhood. She kept busy until her death, performing over 70 concerts yearly. Guy made Chicago his home for over 50 years. His club, Buddy Guy's Legends, is one of Chicago's most requested destinations by international tourists. Talks are in the works to turn the late Muddy Waters's home, located on the South Side, into a museum. For decades, the home has been a frequent tourist stop for blues fans.

For over 30 years, hundreds of blues artists have performed at the annual Chicago Blues Festival. Today, it is the world's largest free blues festival, attracting more than 500,000 blues lovers annually. On South Michigan Avenue, the famous Chess Records building, where many blues musicians recorded, is now the home of the Willie Dixon's Blues Heaven Foundation. On February 21, 2012, Pres. Barack Obama and First Lady Michelle Obama hosted "In Performance at the White House: Red, White, and Blues." That evening, Buddy Guy and B.B. King sang "Sweet Home Chicago" with the president.

On February 21, 2012, the White House hosted a blues celebration event. This photograph shows Pres. Barack Obama singing with B.B. King. Also onstage are, from left to right, Troy "Trombone Shorty" Andrews, Jeff Beck, Derek Trucks, and Gary Clark Jr. They are performing Chicago's signature song, "Sweet Home Chicago." (Official White House Photo, Bob Mehr.)

This is the official 2013 Chicago Blues Festival poster. The theme for this, the 30th annual festival, was a musical journey up the Mississippi—Rollin' Up the River. Headliners included Shemekia Copeland, Bobby Rush, Irma Thomas, the Bar-Kays, Eddie Floyd, Otis Clay, James Cotton, Lil' Ed, and Billy Branch. (City of Chicago Department of Cultural Affairs and Special Events.)

In 1936, George "Buddy" Guy was born in Lettsworth, Louisiana. Raised there, he came to Chicago in 1957. He played guitar in Muddy Waters's band for years and was a house guitarist at Chess Records. For over 50 years, Buddy's career as a blues artist has continued to expand. He is a six-time Grammy winner and was among those awarded the 2012 Kennedy Center Honors. (Chicago History Museum.)

Buddy Guy's Legends continues to be used for live recordings. Blues groups such as father and son Carey (b. 1936) and Lurrie (b. 1958) Bell have recorded here. Sadly, Carey passed away in 2007. (Chicago History Museum.)

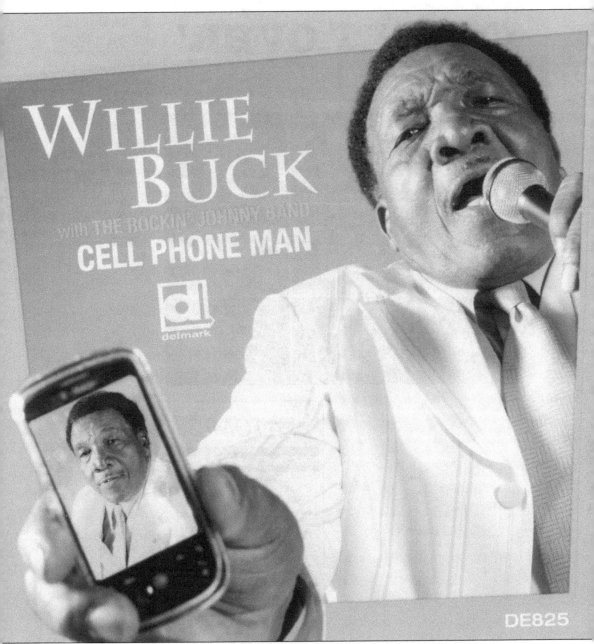

Veteran blues singer Willie Buck was born in 1937 in the small town of Houston, Mississippi. He migrated to Chicago in 1954 and was a regular performer on Maxwell Street. Buck has reinvented his style of blues singing over the years. His first recording was in the 1970s, titled "The Disco Blues." In 2012, he released the album *Cell Phone Man*, which received rave reviews from music critics. In 2004, Buck was inducted into the Chicago Blues Hall of Fame. (Delmark Records.)

IT AIN'T OVER!

DELMARK CELEBRATES 55 YEARS OF BLUES
AT BUDDY GUY'S LEGENDS IN CHICAGO

LURRIE BELL / JIMMY JOHNSON / ZORA YOUNG / TAIL DRAGGER / LITTLE ARTHUR DUNCAN
AARON MOORE / EDDIE SHAW / DAVE SPECTER / SHIRLEY JOHNSON >> LIVE ON STAGE!

It 2012, Delmark Records celebrated its 55th anniversary by releasing a DVD recorded at Buddy Guy's Legends. Lurrie Bell, Tail Dragger, Zora Young, Jimmy Johnson with Dave Specter, Aaron Moore, Little Arthur Duncan, Eddie Shaw, and Shirley Johnson participated, performing some of their signature songs. (Delmark Records.)

Amy O'Neal started a popular late-night blues radio show in the 1970s. It was called *Atomic Mama's Wang-Dang-Doodle Blues Show*. O'Neal interviewed some of the biggest blues artists, played their songs, and promoted their events on her show. (Chicago History Museum.)

ATOMIC MAMA'S
wang-dang-doodle
BLUES SHOW

live music, interviews,
and dusty records from the 20's to the 70's

thurs. nights at 11 pm

WNIB, 97.1 fm

BIG TOWN PRODUCTIONS

★ ★ PRESENTS ★ ★

CHICAGO'S BLUES ALL-STARS

BIG WALTER HORTON - EDDIE TAYLOR
FLOYD JONES - SAM LAY

M. C., AMY "ATOMIC MAMA" O'NEAL

★ ★ **TWO NIGHTS ONLY** ★ ★

FRIDAY, AUGUST 9

8:00 P. M. TO 1:00 A. M.

SATURDAY, AUGUST 10

8:00 P. M. TO 2.00 A. M.

—AT—

KING'S CLUB WAVELAND

3658 NORTH SOUTHPORT

ADVANCE TICKETS $2.00 AT JAZZ RECORD MARTS, 7 W. GRAND AND 4243 N. LINCOLN
$2.50 AT DOOR

Amy "Atomic Mama" O'Neal was a great promoter of blues events. This 1970s poster advertises a two-day blues concert. Listed here are some of the best blues artists of that period: Big Walter Horton, Eddie Taylor, Floyd Jones, and Sam Lay. (Chicago History Museum.)

"Little" Arthur Duncan (1934–2008) was one of America's best electric bluesmen. He was a harmonica player, singer, and songwriter. Born in Indianola, Mississippi, he moved to Chicago at the age of 16 and worked with Little Walter and Jimmy Reed. Eventually, Duncan went solo and performed in and around the Chicago area. Through the 1960s and 1970s, he kept his steady construction job during the day and sang the blues at night. (Delmark Records.)

Little Arthur Duncan's final recording was 2007's *Live at Rosa's Blues Lounge*. He died the following year at the age of 74 from complications following brain surgery. (Delmark Records.)

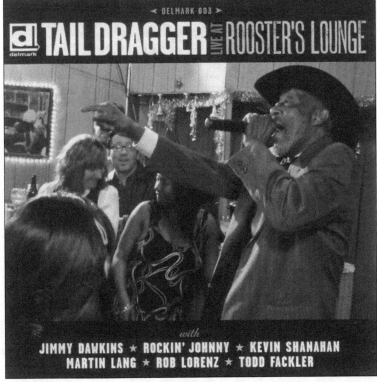

Tail Dragger (James Yancey Jones) has been singing the blues since the 1960s. He was born in Altheimer, Arkansas, in 1940, and he grew up there. He moved to Chicago's West Side to pursue his blues career in 1966. (Delmark Records.)

It was rumored that blues artist Howlin' Wolf gave James Yancy Jones his stage name, Tail Dragger, because he often arrived late for his performances. (Chicago History Museum.)

Tail Dragger fans often describe his style of blues playing as lowdown and dirty, real-deal Chicago blues. Critics describe his music as emotional, intense, and raw, with no apologies. (Delmark Records.)

Some of the best blues performers worked on the streets at the Maxwell Street Market on Chicago's West Side. These amateur musicians and performers put their hearts and souls into their acts for pocket change from the listening crowds. (Chicago History Museum.)

Many blues artists were discovered at the Maxwell Street Market. Record company executives, booking agents, and club promoters often visited this marketplace to search for new talent. (Chicago History Museum.)

Amateur groups designed and used unique items to create their signature blues sounds. This old washboard, along with the triangle, bell, and wash pan, probably produced a Mississippi Delta blues sound. (Chicago History Museum.)

Some of the best harmonica players could be found at the Maxwell Street Market. Many of them migrated from the Mississippi Delta, where this instrument, along with the guitar, was essential for playing Delta-style blues. (Chicago History Museum.)

Maxwell Street Market has always been a place with a tolerance for people from all walks of life. They could come and haggle over goods, listen to great music, and enjoy foods that have been prepared and served the same way for almost a century. (Chicago History Museum.)

This photograph of Koko Taylor (1928–2009) was taken at the height of her career. She was given the title "Queen of the Blues." In 1965, Taylor recorded "Wang Dang Doodle," which was written by Willie Dixon. The following year, it sold over a million copies. This song became Taylor's signature for the remainder of her life. (Chicago History Museum.)

Electric blues guitarist, singer, and songwriter Johnny B. Moore was born in Clarksdale, Mississippi, in 1950. He was influenced by John Lee Hooker, Jimmy Reed, Magic Sam, and Muddy Waters. In the 1970s, Moore was a member of Koko Taylor's band. Since 1987, he has released nine solo albums. In 2001, Moore recorded the album *Born in Clarksdale, Mississippi*. The album's 12 songs pay homage to his birthplace, Clarksdale. A few of the songs, such as "Elmore James Medley," "170 Pounds of Joy," and "Legends of the Blues" are classics. (Delmark Records.)

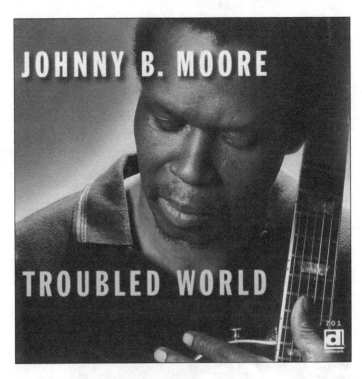

In 1948, blues singer Zora Young was born in West Point, Mississippi. At the age of seven, she moved to Chicago with her family. As a professional blues singer, she has toured Europe over 30 times, and she has performed in Turkey and Taiwan. She has performed at the Annual Chicago Blues Festival six times. Young also had the awesome opportunity to be cast in the role of Bessie Smith in the stage show *The Heart of the Blues*. (Delmark Records.)

Chicago-based Delta blues singer Jimmy Burns was born in 1943 in Dublin, Mississippi. At the age of 12, he moved with his family to Chicago. Throughout the 1960s, Burns mostly recorded as a solo artist. (Both, Delmark Records.)

Two of Jimmy Burn's signature records are "I Really Love You" (1972, Erica Records) and "Can't Get Over" (Dispo Records). Today, he continues to tour nationally and internationally. (Delmark Records.)

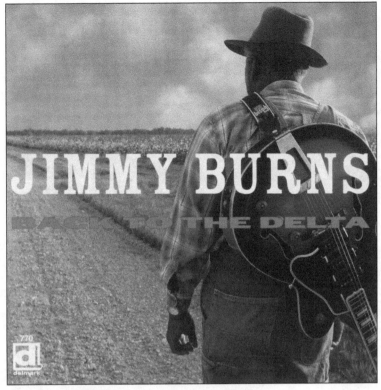

Otis Rush was born in 1935 in Philadelphia, Mississippi, and migrated to Chicago in 1948. His powerful tenor voice won him a Grammy for best traditional blues album for *Any Place I'm Going* (House of Blues) in 1998. (Delmark Records.)

MAGIC SLIM & THE TEARDROPS
JOE CARTER WITH SUNNYLAND SLIM

that ain't right

786

Magic Slim (Morris Holt, 1937–2013) was an American blues singer and guitarist. He was born in Torrance, Mississippi. In 1955, he followed the example of Muddy Waters and Howlin' Wolf, coming to Chicago to pursue his music career. However, it was not until 1966 that Slim recorded his first song, "Scufflin'." His first album, *Born Under a Bad Sign*, was recorded in 1977 for the French label MCM. (Delmark Records.)

Chicago blues singer Bonnie Lee (Jessie Lee Frealls, 1931–2006) was born in Bunkie, Louisiana. She was known as the "Sweetheart of the Blues." She moved to Chicago in 1958 and chose the stage name Bonnie Lee. In 1967, she first appeared on the bill with pianist Sunnyland Slim. They worked many of the local Chicago blues clubs. In 1982, she partnered with Big Time Sarah and Zora Young; the trio called themselves Blues with the Girls. After a series of illnesses, Lee died in 2006 at the age of 75. (Delmark Records.)

Blues singer, bassist, and songwriter Willie Kent (1936–2006) was born in Inverness, Sunflower County, Mississippi. In over 50 years, he recorded 12 albums and performed frequently in Chicago blues clubs. In 2004, Kent recorded his last album, *Blues and Trouble* (Isabel Records). He was diagnosed with colon cancer and died in 2006. Kent will be forever remembered for the styles of blues he mastered—modern electric Chicago blues, regional blues, and modern electric blues. (Delmark Records.)

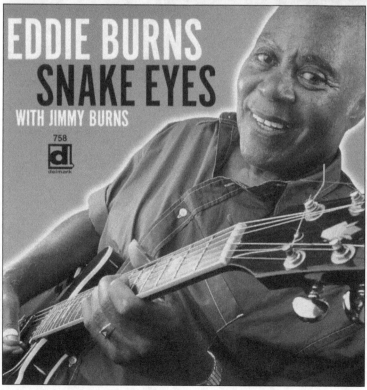

Harmonica player, singer, and songwriter Eddie "Guitar" Burns was born in 1928 in Belzoni, Mississippi. His was influenced by Big Bill Broonzy and Sonny Boy Williamson. In 1948, Burns moved to Detroit and performed locally. It was not until 1972 that Burns undertook a European tour and recorded his first album, *Bottle Up & Go*, in London, England. He was the brother of blues artist Jimmy Burns. (Both, Delmark Records.)

Blues artist Mighty Joe Young
(Joseph Young, 1927–1999) was
born in Shreveport, Louisiana, but
he was raised in Milwaukee. In the
1960s, he started with blues greats
such as Otis Rush, Magic Sam, and
Jimmy Rogers. One of Young's songs,
"Turning Point," is featured in the
Michael Mann movie *Thief* (1981).
Young died from complications
from surgery. (Delmark Records.)

In 1999, the City of Chicago
Department of Cultural Affairs erected
this marker in front of the home of
the late Muddy Waters. It gives a
summary of the bluesman's extensive
career, from working as a sharecropper
in Mississippi to becoming one of
the world's greatest blues artists.
(Photograph by Antoinette Simpson.)

The Muddy Waters home is located at 4339 South Lake Park Avenue, in the Kenwood neighborhood, on Chicago's South Side. It was built in 1879 and designed as a two-unit apartment building. (Photograph by Antoinette Simpson.)

Muddy Waters purchased this home in 1954 and stayed in it for 20 years. He entertained some of the greatest performers of that time, including Chuck Berry and Howlin' Wolf. (Photograph by Antoinette Simpson.)

For more than 25 years, the Muddy Waters home has been vacant. It was placed on the endangered list of properties facing possible demolition. In January 2014, it was purchased by an anonymous buyer who plans to turn it into a museum paying homage to Waters. (Photograph by Antoinette Simpson.)

This sculpture of a blues singer is located at Forty-seventh Street and Martin Luther King Jr. Drive in Bronzeville. Recently, this area was designated as the Chicago Blues District. The district includes statues of an electric guitarist, a saxophone player, and a trumpeter. Decades ago, Bronzeville was filled with venues that hosted blues artists. (Photograph by Antoinette Simpson.)

CELEBRATE CHICAGO BLUES

An Urban Experience With

LEGENDARY ALL STARS

★ ★ ★ MARCH ★ ★ ★
18 - "DELTA BLUES"
25 - "CLASSIC BLUES"

★ ★ ★ APRIL ★ ★ ★
1 - "TRIBUTE TO TAMPA"
15 - "POST WAR BLUES"
22 - "CHICAGO! BLUES! TODAY!"
26 - "BLUE MONDAY"

LIVE AT THE CHECKERBOARD LOUNGE

PARTIALLY FUNDED BY THE ILLINOIS ART COUNCIL

REGISTER NOW!
Loyola University Program For Continuing Education
★ ★ ★ 670-3014 ★ ★ ★

Blues programs and events were advertised in a variety of ways. This special invitation promotes weeks of blues events and excellent artists at the renowned Checkerboard Lounge. (Chicago History Museum.)

The renowned Checkerboard Lounge selected Syl Johnson and Buddy Guy to celebrate its 11th anniversary in 1983. The original location of this lounge was opened in 1972 by L.C. Thurman and Buddy Guy, at 443 East Forty-third Street. The biggest, most renowned performance at the Checkerboard took place on November 22, 1981, when Muddy Waters and the Rolling Stones performed together onstage. Guy remained a partner until 1986. (Chicago History Museum.)

CHECKERBOARD LOUNGE
423 EAST 43rd STREET
CELEBRATING 11th YEAR
Anniversary
AUG. 26-27-28
FRIDAY, SATURDAY, SUNDAY
SHOWTIME: 9:00 P. M. UNTIL
WITH BLUES RECORDING ARTIST

SYL JOHNSON
AND HIS REVUE

Performing Such Hits as "Sock It To Me"
"Take Me to the River" - "Is It Because I'm Black"
"Bring Out the Blues In Me" and Many More

SPECIAL GUEST BUDDY GUY
PHONE: 373-5948

116

In 2005, L.C. Thurman, along with the assistance of the University of Chicago, relocated the Checkerboard Lounge to a more spacious and comfortable building, at 5201 South Harper Court, in the Hyde Park neighborhood. (Photograph by Antoinette Simpson.)

In its new location, the lounge was renamed the New Checkerboard Lounge. Performers from around the world come here to play music, not just blues and jazz. Rock bands and country-music artists have graced the stage. (Photograph by Antoinette Simpson.)

This building was the home of the famous Chess Records, which was located at 2120 South Michigan Avenue, from 1956 to 1965. Brothers Leonard (1927–1969) and Phil Chess (b. 1921) formed and ran Chess Records, which specialized in a variety of music, including rhythm and blues, soul, early rock 'n' roll, and jazz. However, it was the blues artists that drew attention to Chess Records. Willie Dixon, Muddy Waters, Bo Diddley, Little Walter, Chuck Berry, and Howlin' Wolf are just a few of the artists who recorded with Chess. (Photograph by Antoinette Simpson.)

Today, the Chess Records building is the home of Willie Dixon's Blues Heaven Foundation. The foundation's mission is to help artists and musicians obtain an understanding of the music industry and to educate adults and children about the history of the blues. (Photograph by Antoinette Simpson.)

On May 16, 1990, the City of Chicago granted the Chess Records building landmark status. However, over the years, the Blues Heaven Foundation has incurred some financial difficulties. Willie Dixon's royalty income has been used to keep the foundation alive. Dixon wrote Muddy Waters's signature song, "Hoochie Coochie Man," "Back Door Man," and hundreds of other songs. (Photograph by Antoinette Simpson.)

This sign is located at 2120 South Michigan Avenue, in front of the Chess Records building. It showcases a time line of important events that took place within Chess Records. Persons shown on the mural include Leonard and Phil Chess, Willie Dixon, Muddy Waters, and Chuck Berry. (Photograph by Antoinette Simpson.)

Located next to the Willie Dixon's Blues Heaven Foundation is Willie Dixon's Blues Garden. It has an open-air performance stage and is surrounded by banners and silhouettes of famous blues performers, including Koko Taylor, John Lee Hooker, and Willie Dixon. The garden is used for summer concerts, music education programs, and special events. (Photograph by Antoinette Simpson.)

When blues concerts are held in Willie Dixon's Blues Garden, there is always a packed and enthusiastic audience. (Photograph by Antoinette Simpson.)

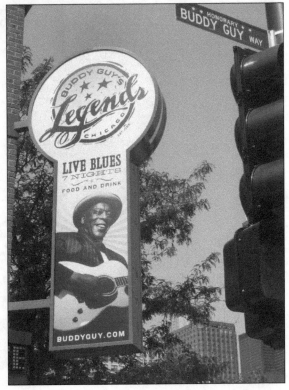

Buddy Guy's Legends has been open since 1989. In 2010, it moved to this location at 700 South Wabash Avenue. Without question, this is one of the biggest tourist attractions in Chicago. (Photograph by Antoinette Simpson.)

Guests who come to Buddy Guy's Legends can enjoy some of the best live music in the world for a mere $10 or $20 per person. This is one of the few places to experience live blues seven nights a week. Occasionally, Buddy Guy surprises the guests and performs himself. There is no dress code, and reservations are not accepted. (Photograph by Antoinette Simpson.)

The menu at Buddy Guy's Legends includes Southern, Cajun, and soul food. Cajun dishes include gumbo, Cajun popcorn, etouffee, jambalaya, red beans, catfish po'boy, and Bourbon Street pecan pie. These dishes are links to Guy's childhood, when he lived in Louisiana. (Photograph by Antoinette Simpson.)

The Chicago Blues Festival was founded in 1983 by the City of Chicago. This three-day festival remains the largest free blues event in the world, and it is the largest music festival in Chicago. (City of Chicago.)

Blues musician Robert Johnson wrote the song "Sweet Home Chicago" in 1937. The city, known for making no small plans, adopted this blues song, which remains Chicago's most popular anthem. (Carol M. Highsmith Archive, Library of Congress, Prints and Photographs Division.)

During the three-day blues festival, more than 500,000 blues fans enjoy performances on five stages. Some of the biggest artists in the industry have graced the stage, including B.B. King, Buddy Guy, Koko Taylor, and Bonnie Raitt. (City of Chicago Department of Cultural Affairs and Special Events.)

"The blues is . . . where we came from and what we experience. . . . The blues came from nothingness, from want, from desire," said W.C. Handy (1873–1958). (Carol M. Highsmith Archive, Library of Congress, Prints and Photographs Division.)

ABOUT THE AUTHOR

Wilbert Jones is president of the Chicago-based Wilbert Jones Company. He is a lover of food and music, especially the blues. Jones has authored several cookbooks and was the host of the 2008 PBS television series *Healthy Heritage Kitchen*. He also coauthored Images of America: *Chicago's Gold Coast*, about his neighborhood in Chicago. (Photograph by Antoinette Simpson.)

Visit us at
arcadiapublishing.com